21st
Century
Skills Library

COOL ARTS CAREERS

ACTOR

BARBARA A. SOMERVILL

Published in the United States of America by
Cherry Lake Publishing, Ann Arbor, Michigan
www.cherrylakepublishing.com

Content Adviser
Brian Shaw, MA, Professor, Theater Department, Columbia College Chicago

Photo Credits
Cover and page 1, ©Allstar Picture Library/Alamy; page 4, ©Paul Doyle/Alamy; page 7,
©Peter Lovás/Dreamstime.com; page 9, ©Adam Eastland Rome/Alamy; page 10,
©Bidouze Stéphane/Dreamstime.com; page 12, ©Joyce Michaud/Dreamstime.com;
page 15, ©Sean De Burca/Shutterstock, Inc.; page 16, ©iStockphoto.com/izusek;
page 17, ©Gynane/Dreamstime.com; page 18, ©Piero Cruciatti/Dreamstime.com;
page 19, ©Blend Images/Alamy; page 20, ©Darwin Lopez/Dreamstime.com;
page 24, ©Photolibrary; page 28, ©Denis Makarenko/Dreamstime.com

Library of Congress Cataloging-in-Publication Data
Somervill, Barbara A.
  Actor/by Barbara A. Somervill.
     p. cm.—(Cool arts careers)
  Includes bibliographical references and index.
  ISBN-13: 978-1-61080-129-4 (lib. bdg.)
  ISBN-10: 1-61080-129-6 (lib. bdg.)
1. Motion picture acting—Vocational guidance—Juvenile literature.
2. Television acting—Vocational guidance—Juvenile literature. I. Title. II. Series.
  PN1995.9.A26S67 2012
  791.4302'8023—dc22   2011001167

Cherry Lake Publishing would like to acknowledge
the work of The Partnership for 21st Century Skills.
Please visit www.21stcenturyskills.org for more information.

Printed in the United States of America
Corporate Graphics Inc.
July 2011
CLFA09

COOL ARTS CAREERS

TABLE OF CONTENTS

CHAPTER ONE
A DAY AT WORK

Actors work on plays, movies, and television shows. They provide **narration** for **documentaries**, appear in commercials, and read aloud to record audiobooks.

Actors play a wide variety of roles on the stage and screen.

Some actors become major stars, but many do not. Instead, they work a variety of interesting jobs. Actors may work on cruise lines, in theme parks, or at fairs and festivals. They **audition** for roles. They might teach acting at schools, parks, or community centers.

Ed Gero is a professor at George Mason University and a **professional** actor. He is playing the role of Scrooge in a stage production of *A Christmas Carol*. Gero juggles his teaching duties at the university with **rehearsals** and **performances**.

21ST CENTURY CONTENT

In the past 10 years, the popularity of video games has opened up new opportunities for actors. Many modern games include complex stories with many characters. Actors are called on to do **voice-over** work for the characters. It may take an actor less than an hour to read all the lines a character might say throughout a game, or it may take several days. Some actors create unique voices for several different characters. It is interesting work, and it pays well. It can also lead to more work if a new version of the game is made.

Gero pays attention to his makeup and costume. He runs through his lines in his head. He must become Scrooge. "On stage, it's all you," he says. "The performance depends on you, and there are no second takes." Even though he has played Scrooge many times, Gero puts special care into every performance. He knows that people in today's audience may be seeing *A Christmas Carol* for the first time. They deserve his best work.

Kate Kiley adjusts her headphones and gets ready to begin recording. She is a professional actor who reads books for the Library of Congress's National Library Service for the Blind and Physically Handicapped. Even though she's not onstage, she is still acting. "When you read a book for the blind, your voice has to communicate everything. You have to create different roles, personalities, and emotions just with your voice," says Kiley. "On one page, I might have to play a grandmother, a father, and a child. The people who listen to these books need to see the story through my reading."

Recording audiobooks is not easy. "You learn as you go," Kiley explains. "You do your homework, learn how to pronounce specific words or names, and you rehearse on your own. You can't waste recording time with rereads of the same material." Kiley reads both adult and children's books. She enjoys the challenge and variety of her job.

Some actors play characters in theme parks.

Hank Stone is on his way to a night shoot near Tampa, Florida. Stone teaches speech and theater at Seminole State College of Florida and schedules movie roles in between his teaching duties. After driving nearly 2 hours, he gets to the **location** in time for makeup, costuming, and instructions from the director. The shoot runs all night, and Stone heads back to school in the early hours of the morning.

He teaches his morning classes and heads home for a nap. By 6:00 p.m., he'll be on the road back to the shoot's location. Stone believes the long travel times and lack of sleep are worth the reward. "Everything is about a brilliant performance," he says. "You must really have the spirit of creative energy and enthusiasm, or you won't go far in acting."

LIFE & CAREER SKILLS

Many people continue their education even after they have become successful at their jobs. Actors are no different. Even experienced actors go back to school. Many actors take master classes in stage fighting, movement, voice, and other important skills. These classes are not usually open to the public. Actors may have to audition for a place in a class, and serious actors always do their homework.

Film sets are busy places.

CHAPTER TWO
LEARNING TO PERFORM

The best place to start an acting career is in school. Become involved with your school's drama program. Audition for every play. If you don't get a role, work backstage painting sets or doing lighting. Every production depends on teamwork, and every production you work on increases your knowledge of acting.

Lighting and sets are just as important as performances in a stage play.

Working backstage helps actors learn their craft. "When I was in high school, I played an assortment of roles in plays and musicals, but I also worked backstage and observed everything," says Kiley. "How did that actor move across the stage, engage the audience? Every play was a chance to learn something new."

Working on plays is also a great way to make friends. According to Gero, "The theater was the place where I found friendships. I found my future through the arts, not on the sports field." He adds, "If you want to be an actor, play. Participate. It doesn't matter the size of the part you play. Every job you do will make you a better actor."

LIFE & CAREER SKILLS

For many young actors, drama school is the next step after high school. To get spots in most good drama schools, students must present audition pieces. They choose lines from favorite plays and perform them in front of teachers from the school. Libraries often have books filled with excellent audition pieces. Auditioning actors might prepare one classic speech and another from a modern play. They might also choose pieces that show off their different abilities, such as comic or dramatic acting.

Education is important for any actor. Actors need to know about history, music, art, and literature. They need to complete high school and develop their skills in college or drama school. They study speech, dance, Shakespeare, and modern theater. Many schools also offer classes on film and video work, **stagecraft**, and directing.

Learning to direct can help make you a better actor.

Talent, good looks, and a pleasant voice are helpful for actors, but other skills are even more important. Actors need to be observant. This helps them learn about people's emotions and attitudes. Learn to observe others, both on and off stage. This will help you to better understand the ways people behave in real life. It will also help you understand what natural **dialogue** sounds like.

LEARNING & INNOVATION SKILLS

Building a **network** makes it easier to develop a successful acting career. The Internet is a key factor in finding jobs. You can find listings for auditions, get e-mails about upcoming shows or movie shoots, and learn about drama school programs. Social networks and Web sites can showcase your work. Keep in touch with people you work with on different shows. They can let you know about new opportunities, and you can do the same for them.

Curiosity is important, too. The more you learn about your craft, the better your acting will become. You need to be curious about the world around you as well. Learn about other cultures and their customs. Apply that knowledge to your acting. Actors also need to use their imaginations. They imagine ways that their characters might react to different situations. This helps them find interesting ways to approach a role.

LEARNING & INNOVATION SKILLS

Actors memorize their lines in many different ways. Some actors learn best by reading their lines. Others need to hear the lines aloud. Record your lines so you can listen to them while doing other things. Some actors need to perform the lines themselves. Ask a friend to help you perform a short piece of a play. Hearing your friend's lines might help you remember what to say next. Which way is best at helping you learn lines? Once you figure it out, you'll be one step further on the path to becoming a successful actor.

CASTING →

Working with fellow actors is a great way to learn lines.

Actors need to be determined. "You need to get used to rejection," says Kiley. "You may audition dozens of times and only get a few roles." Keep trying. You may be rejected for reasons that have nothing to do with your acting skills. Directors may want someone with a certain age, race, or height for a role. You cannot make yourself 6 inches taller or 30 years older.

Have respect for the actors, directors, and technicians you work with. Show up for rehearsals on time. Learn your lines and pay attention to the director's instructions. Learn about the time period, the clothing, and the social manners

◀ CASTING   ◀ CASTING

Being prepared for auditions is important.

Some actors specialize in recreating certain time periods.

of the play's setting. Doing these things will help you develop a solid work ethic. "I want to work with people who are as serious about the work as I am," says Gero.

Not everyone can be a star. Sometimes, smaller roles
are the best parts of a play or a movie. Think of Professor
Snape in the *Harry Potter* movies, the Wicked Witch in
The Wizard of Oz, or Lewbert the Doorman in *iCarly*.
Although these parts may be small, they are just as
important as the main characters.

Not everyone is cut out for being on stage or in front of the
camera. These people can still get jobs in theater, movies, or
television. They might be set designers or lighting technicians.
They might become directors, writers, or costume designers.
Special effects and stunts play an important role in many of
today's movies. These jobs all require education, training, and
experience. You can begin getting experience through school,
college, or a community theater.

*Some people enjoy being behind the
camera more than being in front of it.*

Every part, no matter how small or large, is an opportunity to develop your acting skills.

CHAPTER THREE
THE DEMANDS OF ACTING

Acting is rarely a Monday-to-Friday, nine-to-five job. Actors work nights and weekends. They work through cold, rain, and strong winds. Their jobs might take them to foreign countries. Hours can be long. Television and movie actors might need to do the same scenes over and over.

People come from around the world to see Broadway plays.

Actors might wait around for long periods of time to do a scene that requires only a minute or two of acting. Jobs may take one day, several months, or even years.

Most actors have long periods when they are out of work. Many take on other jobs to help pay the bills. A television commercial takes a day or two to shoot. It takes several weeks or months to shoot a movie. Unless you are one of the stars, you would only work part of that time. Broadway plays and touring companies provide jobs for months and even years. It can be challenging to perform the same role hundreds of times and always play it as though it were opening night.

21ST CENTURY CONTENT

The aliens in *Avatar* were not played by tall, blue actors with tails. Instead, these roles were played by actors wearing motion capture suits. Motion capture suits are covered with hundreds of tiny sensors that record an actor's movements. Even the actors' mouths, eyes, and other facial features were closely monitored. Computers used the human actors' movements to create the aliens. While actors Zoe Saldana and Sam Worthington looked nothing like their alien characters, their acting skills made the creatures more realistic.

Most professional actors belong to unions. Most high-paying acting jobs are union jobs, so membership is required to get work. The Screen Actors Guild (SAG) is the union for movie actors, while the American Federation of Television and Radio Artists (AFTRA) covers radio and television performers. The Actors' Equity Association (AEA) is the union for stage actors. "If you want to have an acting career, you have to have the union card," says Kate Kiley. "Without it, you just can't get paying jobs."

In 2008, there were about 56,500 jobs for actors. The median wage for actors was $16.59 per hour. In 2009, actors who had speaking parts in movies or on television got paid at least $782 per day or $2,713 for a five-day week. It is difficult to figure out a realistic average for actors' wages because a select few earn so much money. A star might earn $20 million for a role in a blockbuster movie. There are nearly 100,000 SAG members, but only 50 to 75 of them earn such high salaries.

Actors learn to market their skills in many ways. They might do voice-overs for commercials, documentaries, or industrial videos. Summer work at theme parks or on cruise lines pays well and offers travel, a room, and food in addition to pay. Modeling pays well and gives actors a chance to be seen by large audiences.

Acting in commercials is a great way for actors to earn money. Advertising agencies hire actors to do commercials for television, radio, and the Internet. National commercials usually pay much better than local ones. Some commercials pay a set amount. Others pay the actors a small amount of money every time the commercial is shown. For a national commercial, that can add up to a big paycheck.

LEARNING & INNOVATION SKILLS

Teaching is one way for actors to earn a steady paycheck. High school, college, and drama school teachers all need college degrees. They train students for a future as professional actors. Other actors bring their knowledge to people at hospitals, parks, or even prisons. They help people learn to act for fun or to express their feelings. It is possible to have a successful career as an actor and also teach. Ed Gero and Hank Stone are both teachers and actors.

CHAPTER FOUR
ACTING IN THE FUTURE

F ew jobs are as **competitive** as acting. The Screen Actors Guild has about 100,000 members. The Actors' Equity Association lists about 48,000 members. The American Federation of Television and Radio Artists has 70,000 members. Some actors may belong to more than one group, and not all of the members are active actors. The majority of them do not work more than a month or two a year as actors.

Most actors work other jobs to help support themselves between acting jobs.

Most professional film and television work is done in New York and Los Angeles. In the past 10 years, independent films and cable stations have provided more work in other cities. Movies are shot on location throughout the world. The Canadian cities of Vancouver and Toronto have become popular places to shoot television shows and movies.

Professional theaters offering paid positions can be found in most large cities. Chicago, Boston, Philadelphia, and many others all have active, paid theater groups. Summer stock theater, Shakespeare festivals, and small theater companies offer seasonal work. Productions in large theaters usually pay more because they draw a larger paying audience.

LEARNING & INNOVATION SKILLS

William Shakespeare never goes out of style. Most of his plays are performed over and over again every year. Actors and directors continue to find new ways of making the material exciting. It is a good idea for young actors to learn about these classic plays. Summer camps and festivals are great opportunities for beginning actors to learn about classical theater. The best ones, such as the Oregon Shakespeare Festival, feature both professional and amateur actors. You can learn a lot about acting from watching how different actors play Shakespeare's classic characters. Look for a Shakespeare festival near you and get involved.

There will continue to be film, television, and theater roles for beginning actors. Film and television need extras, or additional actors, to fill out city and town scenes. Unless the role is a speaking part, it may not be a paying job. Community theater is another opportunity to develop your skills. Summer camps and drama festivals also provide a place to learn more about acting.

The Bureau of Labor Statistics predicts that there will be 63,700 acting jobs available by 2018. That is an increase of about 11 percent over 2008's opportunities. A rising demand in other countries for American films should create more jobs for actors. Cable television, the Internet, and independent movies should also increase the number of jobs available to actors. Getting these jobs will be difficult. Many actors will audition for each role.

Established actors fill most lead roles in television shows and movies. Some of these actors do several jobs in a single year. For example, one actor might act in a television series, commercials, a live play, and a film all in the same year. That these actors fill so many of the biggest roles makes it even more difficult to break into acting.

"A successful acting career depends on the three Es: education, exaltation, and entertainment," says Hank Stone. "You need a broad, solid education in order to understand and play a variety of roles. Exaltation refers to spirit. Your acting needs to stem from a creative spirit, a connection to your inner self. Finally, it is all about entertainment, and that is not your entertainment but the audience's entertainment. Acting is making a connection to other people, bringing them joy, fear, excitement, and sorrow. Learn how to make those connections."

21ST CENTURY CONTENT

Remember that acting is a business. Actors must sell their talent, looks, and personality. Actors who limit their skills to one character type will not get much work. Famous actors such as Glenn Close and Helen Mirren have done drama and comedy. They have played both lead and supporting roles. They do films, television shows, and stage plays. They do voice-overs for animated films and act in Shakespearean plays. The more you can do, the better your chance of selling your acting abilities.

Your school could be holding auditions for its annual play right now. What are you waiting for? Show up and take a chance. Take whatever part you are given and make the most of it. You'll have fun, learn about acting, and make a start on an interesting future. Break a leg!

Will Smith has found great success as an actor in both television and film.

SOME FAMOUS ACTORS

Ben Stiller (1965–) is the son of comedians Jerry Stiller and Anne Meara. He has worked on more than 50 films as an actor, director, writer, and producer. Stiller has won an Emmy and several MTV Movie Awards. He has appeared in *Night at the Museum* and *Tropic Thunder* and is also the voice of Alex the lion in *Madagascar*.

Robert De Niro (1943–) is considered by many to be one of the greatest actors of all time. Since his debut in 1965, he has appeared in more than 80 films, including such classics as *Taxi Driver* (1976), *Raging Bull* (1980), and *Goodfellas* (1990). De Niro has won two Academy Awards and has been nominated for four others.

Katharine Hepburn (1907–2003) began acting in stage plays while she was in college. She soon won roles on Broadway and appeared in her first film in 1932. She went on to star in more than 50 films, winning four Academy Awards and nominations for eight others. No other actress has ever won as many Oscars.

Jane Lynch (1960–) is a comedic actress who has appeared in many films, plays, and TV shows during her long career. She began her career as a stage actress and improv comedian before going on to scene-stealing roles in films such as *Best in Show* (2000) and *Talladega Nights* (2006). She currently stars as Sue Sylvester on the popular TV sitcom *Glee*.

Daniel Radcliffe (1989–) started his career at the age of 10, when he appeared in a TV movie based on Charles Dickens's *David Copperfield*. Two years later, he was cast in the role of Harry Potter. He has since gone on to act in all eight *Harry Potter* films. He has also performed in many stage productions.

Will Smith (1968–) began his career as a rapper called the Fresh Prince. In 1990, he won the lead role in the TV sitcom *The Fresh Prince of Bel-Air*. The show's success launched Smith into a successful movie career. He has acted in such blockbusters as *Independence Day* (1996), *Men in Black* (1997), and *Hitch* (2005).

GLOSSARY

audition (aw-DISH-uhn) to give a trial performance so others can decide if the actor is right for the job

competitive (kahm-PEH-tih-tiv) where multiple people are trying to get the same job or honor

dialogue (DYE-uh-lawg) speech between two or more characters

documentaries (dahk-yuh-MEN-tur-eez) films that show real events or facts

location (loh-KAY-shuhn) site where filming takes place

narration (nar-A-shuhn) spoken words that help to tell the story in a film or television show

network (NET-wurk) a group of people who share professional or social information with one another

performances (per-FOR-muhns-iz) theatrical events

professional (pruh-FESH-uh-nuhl) done for money

rehearsals (ri-HUR-suhlz) practice performances

stagecraft (STAYJ-kraft) the effective management of theatrical devices or techniques

voice-over (VOIS-oh-ver) a performance where an actor provides the voice for an animated character

FOR MORE INFORMATION

BOOKS

Albert, Lisa Rondinelli. *So You Want to Be a Film or TV Actor?* Berkeley Heights, NJ: Enslow Publishers, 2008.

Levy, Frederick. *Acting in Young Hollywood: A Career Guide for Kids, Teens, and Adults Who Play Young, Too.* New York: Watson-Guptill, 2009.

Mayfield, Katherine. *Acting A to Z: The Young Person's Guide to a Stage or Screen Career.* New York: Back Stage Books, 2007.

Rauf, Don, and Monique Vescia. *Actor.* New York: Ferguson Publishing, 2009.

WEB SITES

Globe Theatre Actors
www.globe-theatre.org.uk/globe-theatre-actors.htm
Take a trip into history, and learn about the actors who worked with Shakespeare and played famous Shakespearean roles.

Screen Actors Guild: Day in the Life of a Voice Actor
www.sag.org/day-life-a-voice-actor
Watch a video to find out what a day for a voice actor is like.

Theatre Acting Tips
www.musicaltheatreaudition.com/performance/acting/index.html
Get tips about performing, auditioning, and learning the mechanics of acting.

U.S. Bureau of Labor Statistics—Occupational Outlook Handbook: Actors, Producers, and Directors
www.bls.gov/oco/ocos093.htm
Learn more about what it means to be an actor.

INDEX

ABOUT THE AUTHOR

Barbara A. Somervill worked as a volunteer for a theater company long before she became a writer. She met some wonderful people, both behind the scenes and on the stage. Two of the actors interviewed for this book, Kate Kiley and Hank Stone, worked with her and went on to become professional actors. She says, "It is so exciting watching Kate on stage or seeing Hank in a movie. The theater gave me friends for a lifetime."